Beats was originally developed with the Arches' Platform 18 Award, and premiered at the Arches Glasgow in April 2012, before transferring to the Traverse Theatre, with the following team:

    Kieran Hurley: writer, performer, co-director

    Julia Taudevin: co-director

    Johnny Whoop: DJ, sound and lighting designer

    Jamie Wardop: VJ, video artist

    Oliver Emanuel: dramaturg

    Adam Thayers: technician and lighting support

It was later remounted by Show and Tell and the Arches at the Pleasance, Edinburgh at the Edinburgh Fringe and for subsequent touring in 2013 with the following team:

    Kieran Hurley: writer, performer, co-director

    Julia Taudevin: co-director

    Johnny Whoop: sound and lighting designer, musical director

    Hushpuppy: DJ

    Jamie Wardop: VJ, video artist

    Adam Thayers: technical stage manager

    Tom Searle: producer

Thanks to Tron Theatre, Traverse Theatre and all the staff at the Arches.

KIERAN HURLEY
Writer, Performer, Co-Director

Kieran is an award-winning writer, performer, and theatre maker based in Glasgow whose work has been presented internationally and throughout the UK. His monologue *Beats* was developed with the Arches Platform 18 Award and was awarded Best New Play at the Critics' Awards for Theatre in Scotland (CATS) before being presented at the Traverse Theatre during the Edinburgh Fringe. Other recent work includes: *Hitch* (Arches, Forest Fringe, CATS Best New Play nominee); *Rantin* (National Theatre of Scotland/The Arches); and a number of short mini-plays including *London 2012: Glasgow* (Theatre Uncut) and *Belcoo* (Royal Court, Open Court Festival). Kieran is currently writer in residence with the National Theatre of Scotland as recipient of the Pearson Playwrights' Scheme bursary.

JULIA TAUDEVIN
Co-Director

As a writer, AJ Taudevin's recent plays include: *Some Other Mother*, which recently premiered at the Traverse Theatre; *The YelloWing* (Scottish Mental Health Arts and Film Festival); *The 12:57* (Theatre Uncut); and *The Jean Jacques Rousseau Show* and *Demons* (Oran Mor). She won the Playwrights' Studio Scotland New Playwrights Award in 2010. As an actor, Julia Taudevin has worked for companies including the National Theatre, the National Theatre of Scotland, Traverse Theatre, Magnetic North, The Arches and Tron Theatre. Julia is also Associate Artist at the Tron Theatre, and is currently on a year-long attachment with the Traverse Theatre as one of the Traverse Fifty. Julia co-directed *Beats* and *Hitch*, both by Kieran Hurley.

JOHNNY WHOOP,
Lighting and Sound Designer, Musical Director

Johnny started DJ'ing at parties across the Glasgow area at the end of the 90's developing his mixing skills and building a solid reputation on the underground party scene. He has been DJ'ing professionally for over 13 years and has held residencies at the renowned Death Disco and Octopussy club nights at the Arches, Glasgow, DJ'ing to thousands of clubbers every week and supporting acts such as 2manyDJ's, Erol Alkan and Felix Da Housecat. As a technician and designer, Johnny has worked in sound and lighting for club, corporate and theatre events, including the Slam Tent at T in the Park. He is regularly requested to work for some of the world's biggest international DJ's and will soon be will travelling to Dubai to work for an international production company. His sound design for *Beats* was nominated for Best Music and Sound at the 2012 Critics' Awards for Theatre Scotland (CATS).

JAMIE WARDROP, Video Artist and VJ

Jamie Wardrop is an artist whose practice encompasses theatre, film, animation and musical composition. He studied acting at the Royal Conservatoire of Scotland where he was awarded The Citizens Award for Best Performance in his final year.

He is a resident VJ for Pressure – the renowned club at The Arches where he creates visuals for some of the biggest names in techno.

Jamie is director of Outlet Arts and Glasgow Theatre Arts Collective, an artist led collective which provides affordable rehearsal space for artists working in the city. Jamie is committed to developing cross-disciplinary creative practice.

HUSHPUPPY, DJ

DJ Hushpuppy (Alan Miller) has been running and playing at clubs in Glasgow for almost 20 years. He was a resident at the Arches-based, London-challenging, super-club Death Disco for five years, ran RPZ (the Glasgow Art School's infamous Thursday night residency) for eight years and currently runs the eclectic club night/radio show night Music Please. In tandem with his night-time DJing career Alan has extensive experience as a press agent working in music, clubbing contemporary art, theatre and performance. For 7 years he was based at the influential agency Mingo PR, with clients including DJ Hell, Peaches, Miss Kitten and Gonzales, before turning freelance in 2005 and forging a reputation in Scotland working with Glasgow International Festival of Visual Art, Edinburgh Arts Festival, dance music festival The Electric Frog and LGBTI arts festival Glasgay.

ADAM THAYERS,
Technical Stage Manager

Adam Thayers is a technical manager and theatre technician from Edinburgh. He started off as a scenic carpenter in London creating sets for primetime television shows with *Big Brother* being his major project year-round. He returned to Scotland and retrained for a year in technical theatre, he went straight into work as a freelancer and has worked as a lighting designer, as a technician, and in technical management over the last 3 years for various venues and production companies across Scotland including The Arches, PASS, Catalyst EPS, Summerhall and Underbelly.

OLIVER EMANUEL,
Dramaturg

Oliver Emanuel is a playwright based in Glasgow. He has written plays for most of the major theatres in Scotland as well as extensively for BBC Radio. Recent work includes: *The Day I Swapped My Dad For Two Goldfish* (National Theatre of Scotland) and *Titus* (Macrobert). Forthcoming work includes: *Dragon* (Vox Motus/ National Theatre of Scotland/ Tianjin's People's Arts Theatre), *The Little Boy That Santa Claus Forgot* (Macrobert), *Prom* (Macrobert), and *Albion Street* (BBC Radio Scotland).
For more information visit: www.oliveremanuel.com

SHOW AND TELL

Show And Tell are producers and publicists for the Summer and Autumn 2013 tour of *Beats*, in association with The Arches, Glasgow. Show And Tell are a London-based, award-winning company founded by Tom Searle in 2007. They produce and develop the work of a wide range of acclaimed comedians and theatre-makers. Awards include: Chortle Award for Best Innovation 2012 (La Concepta), Chortle Award for Best Innovation 2008 (laughterinoddplaces). Notable productions include: *Tony Law: Maximum Nonsense* (Foster's Edinburgh Comedy Award nomination 2012, Chortle Award for Best Show winner 2013; Edinburgh Festival, Soho Theatre, UK Tour), *John Peel's Shed* by John Osborne (Edinburgh Festival, Soho Theatre, UK Tour), *La Concepta* by Simon Munnery (Chortle Award for Best Innovation winner; Edinburgh Festival, Soho Theatre, Melbourne International Comedy Festival).

THE ARCHES

The Arches, one of Europe's leading cultural venues, is both an arts receiving and production house with an international reputation as an exciting hub of ground-breaking creativity. Housed within seven Grade A listed Victorian railway arches in Glasgow city centre, the venue presents a year-round programme of theatre, performance, dance, visual art, live music and club nights. The arts programming team employs calculated risk-taking in all of its creative decisions, nurturing emergent talent and rewarding bold approaches with a supportive environment for further innovation – showcased each autumn at Arches LIVE, a two week long celebration of new, Scottish, contemporary performance talent. Alongside local artists, the Arches presents world-class international artists and companies such as The TEAM, Derevo, Ann Liv Young, Mammalian Diving Reflex, Ontroerend Goed, Akhe, Taylor Mac and Tim Crouch in the venue as part of its annual BEHAVIOUR festival of live performance. The Arches regularly wins awards at the Edinburgh Fringe and tours work internationally – in recent years this has included taking shows to New York, Spoleto Festival, Sao Paolo, National Theatre and the Barbican.

www.thearches.co.uk

BEATS

Kieran Hurley

BEATS

OBERON BOOKS
LONDON

WWW.OBERONBOOKS.COM

First published in 2013 by Oberon Books Ltd
521 Caledonian Road, London N7 9RH
Tel: +44 (0) 20 7607 3637 / Fax: +44 (0) 20 7607 3629
e-mail: info@oberonbooks.com
www.oberonbooks.com

A catalogue record for this book is available from the British Library.

PB ISBN: 978-1-78319-037-9
E ISBN: 978-1-78319-536-7

Cover design Tom Searle / Niall Walker
All images reproduced
by kind permission of Niall Walker / The Arches

Printed and bound in Great Britain by
Marston Book Services Ltd, Oxfordshire

Visit www.oberonbooks.com to read more about all our books and to buy them. You will also find features, author interviews and news of any author events, and you can sign up for e-newsletters so that you're always first to hear about our new releases.

Notes on the original production:

Beats is performed by two performers.

One is an actor, the other is a DJ.

There is also a VJ not visible from the stage, live-mixing video footage which is projected throughout the piece onto a large projector screen on the back wall.

The DJ position is upstage left. Further downstage, and right of centre is a chair at a small wooden desk. On the desk, there is a desk lamp, a microphone, a glass of water and a small round white pill.

The space is filled with a light haze and is lit throughout with moving club lights rather than theatre lights.

The following script contains no sound cues, as the DJ is much more than a sound operator. Though he/she does not necessarily speak the DJ is a constant performing presence and the music should feel organically connected to the narrative throughout. A track list of the music used in the original sound design is featured as an appendix towards the back of this book.

Similarly there are no indications in this script as to the content of the video design, which is live mixed by the VJ, offstage, throughout. The aesthetic of the video should be evocative of early nineties rave culture, loosely illustrating aspects of the story, and, like the music, following its tone and rhythm.

For the sake of this printed version, the names of the actor, DJ, VJ, and lighting operator correspond to those in the original production.

Sometimes scene 2 might contain ad-libbed or improvised moments in response to the mood of the audience.

1.

What do you do when you go out, Johnno?
Where do you go?

I've been hearing stories Johnno, about those
boys, and about drugs. Is there something
you're not telling me son?

Feral. Out of control.

Unless stronger action is taken by the
government these young people will
continue to be a danger to themselves and to
the rest of society.

It doesn't mean nothing.
It doesn't mean nothing.
It doesn't mean nothing.
It doesn't mean nothing.
It doesn't mean.
It means.
It doesn't mean nothing.

2.

Hi

In 1994 the Criminal Justice and Public Order Act made it illegal to have certain gatherings of people around, and this is a quote; 'music wholly or predominantly characterised by the emission of a succession of repetitive beats.'

I'm Kieran. This is Johnny Whoop. And none of this is real.

In a minute I'm going to tell you a story.

Johnny will be playing music. You are a gathering of people. The music that Johnny will be playing can for the most part be characterised by the emission of a succession of repetitive beats.

But this one isn't really real, so we're ok.

Over there are Jamie and Adam. Jamie will be live mixing some video footage like what you just saw on the screen behind me there, and Adam will control the lights. Johnny will play some music, I'll speak some words. And you'll all fill in the gaps.

This is it. This is all there is.

That's your lot, really.

Which is just as well. Because nobody can arrest your imagination. Yet.

And so when I sit down there, the story will begin.

And I need you to imagine a small town in the Central Belt of Scotland, in the mid-1990s. Livingston, as it happens.

I need you to imagine bitumen pavements.
And dog shit. And ten p mixes.

I need you to imagine John Major's Back to
Basics campaign.

I need you to imagine a dreich evening, a
row of hedges, in orange sulphur streetlight.
A small street lined with pebble-dashed flats.

And I need you to imagine a boy's bedroom.
Clothes on the floor. A Super Nintendo
games console with the game Zelda on
pause. A poster of the band the Stone Roses.
On the floor, an empty and broken cassette
case of the hit single *Ebeneezer Goode* by the
Shamen. A faint, but noticeable smell of
Lynx Africa body spray.

And I need you to imagine Johnno
McCreadie.

Johnno is 15 years old.

Small, skinny, shy, and awkward. And full to
bursting of all the raw and holy emotions of
a teenage boy.

His face is a canvas of plooks.

He sits in this bedroom, his bedroom,
looking out the window at the dreich
evening, the orange sulphur streetlight, the
school across the street, the row of hedges,
the bitumen pavements, the dog shit.

Johnno McCreadie, 15 years old:
disappointed with the world, and terrified of
his own place in it; a still-beating heart in a
concrete landscape. A moody wee shite.

3.

Johnno is playing Zelda on the SNES for
about the hundredth time. He's at that
bit where you go into the Dark World for
the first time and turn into a weird pink
bunny rabbit. He's wearing his favourite
green hoody, the one that's too big for him
so when it's pulled up the hood falls right
across his face, keeping him shut off from the
world, separate. He'd taken to wearing it like
that indoors even though in his bedroom the
door to the outside world was always locked.
He'd just had a lock fitted a few months ago
ever since his mum had decided that: you
are at an age now Johnno, where you might
need a bit of, you know. Privacy.

If only she'd buy him one of those new
Playstations. He's been playing this same old
game for about 3 years now. Since he was 12.
Which is basically the same thing as forever.

4.

Alison McCreadie is checking off a list.

Post office. Tick.
Messages. Tick.
Mum's messages. Tick.
Ironing.

Countdown had been on earlier when she got in, kicked off her work shoes, and started making Johnno his tea. Now it was time for that new American show, *Friends*.

Johnno had seemed funny. He wasn't talking. What was the problem?

She's starving. Dinner was the first thing she'd had to eat all day unless you count they two Slim Fast shakes. But she's holding out. She's no going to let a stupid milkshake get the better of her.

She wasnae sure about that *Friends*. All squeaky voices and shiny teeth and flats with purple walls. Purple walls? Was that going to be the new thing? Good grief.

She'd been hearing things. Stories about they boys. She'd have to find a way to talk to him, find out what's going on. He'd think she was getting all worked up for nothing, but she wasn't. She wasn't.

It's no just scare stories Johnno. You don't know it but I've seen some things myself, before you were even around. I'm no daft, son. It's not for no reason that I'm…ach shit.

He'd never listen. He'd never listen to all that. But she'll need to say something, she thinks, she'll need to, as she sits and ticks off

a new list inside her head of all the things
that her wee Johnno might get up to if he
kept hanging around with that crowd.

Dogging school? Probably. Tick.
Fighting? Possibly. Tick.
Drinking? Seemingly. Tick.
Drugs?
Tick. Tick, tick, tick, tick.

5.

Call General Accident Direct on oh eight
hundred one two one double oh four.
You could lower your home contents and
building insurance costs today.

Robert Dunlop stares at the television screen.

Loads of these sortay ads on the telly noo.
Probably worth looking intay, he thinks.
Probably money to be saved somewhere.
Who knows where to start but. Naw. Naw, no
interested thanks.

You are about to experience an impressive
release of power.

Oh aye. Always the same plummy Radio
Four voice an aw. Was that the same guy that
did aw ay these? He's probably making a
racket.

The government will soon be releasing its
remaining shares in National Power and
Powergen.

Shares. Oh right. Probably a good idea,
Robert. You've some money saved after aw.

To register, contact one of the many banks,
building societies, or brokers offering a share
shop service. National Power / Powergen
Share Offer. The Power Issue: Share in it.

Right. Shares. Right maybe. What's this
small print here, the values of shares can
fluctuate any application for, ach shite. Ah
well.

Privatisation Robert, really son?

But that's his Dad talking. That's exactly what his old man would have tae say, the auld idealist. Gies a break Dad. Gies a break ya auld prick I'm 41. And your deid. So get aff ma case.

He'd look into the shares thing later, he thought. Who's stopping him after aw. Naebody. Nae wife nae kids. Naebody that's who.

He chucks a couple of Pro-plus down his neck. Need to wake the system up. Been struggling for sleep since starting these night shifts. Now his old man would have recognised that as good hard work. He just hudnay ever been too keen on the fact that the hard work was being done as a member of the police force.

Ah well. Fuckum.

Later, he'd get ready to go intay the station. Later, he'd get up, heat a tin ay soup, comb his hair, prepare to leave the house. But that was later. For now, there was time for a bit more telly. He'd enjoyed that *Countdown* earlier that was always quite good. She's a good a looking woman that Carol Vorderman. Smart tae. Dunno what she's doing hanging about that Richard Whitely but. Honestly. Prick.

6.

Johnno's walkman headphones dangle
around his neck.

Johnno!

Mum. What does she want? He hates when
she comes into his room so he unlocks the
door, and steps into the hall.

Johnno what are you up to tonight?

Going out later.

Out where Johnno?

Just out.

What do you mean 'just out'?

Dunno.

Johnno, you better not be hanging around
with that Scott Smith again.

How?

Scott Smith is a bad laddie Johnno, I've
heard about him, we all hear all about him
you know that fine well.

You don't even know him Mum.

Scott Smith was Johnno's mate, but
nobody called him Scott Smith. His name
was Spanner. He was 2 years older but
Johnno had been pals with him for years
cos he just lived one block down the road.
Johnno's mum had always been worried
about Spanner leading her wee boy on to
the wrong track, ever since they were wee,
Johnno 9 and Spanner 11, and whenever
Spanner's mum was out they'd sneak into
her kitchen and drink Strongs. A Strong was

when you took a glass and filled it up to the top with diluting juice, and no water. Just the concentrate stuff eh. That's a Strong. Spanner got a bad wrap at school, his whole family did, but he'd always stuck up for Johnno, looked after him, and Johnno was grateful. Johnno liked Spanner. Spanner was a good lad. So everyone else could just Fuck Off.

You don't even know him Mum. He's alright.

What happens when you go out, Johnno? Where do you go? I've been hearing stories Johnno, about those boys, and about, about drugs. Is there something you're not telling me son?

She was just freakin out. All the mums were freakin out these days, ever since all that terrible stuff over at Hangar 13 over in Ayr, and all newspaper headlines about drugs and death. It was actually, when you thought about it, quite scary. It's frustrating but. Johnno wants to talk to her about these things, he does. He wants to say, you know what Mum, I get scared too. I do. But she doesn't understand and he doesn't have the right words to calm her down.

He sticks in his headphones and drowns out his mother's complaints.

Listen here son, you just turn that music off right away! How dare you! I am talking to you!

Johnno turns around, back into his room, and locks the door.

Right you, ya wee shite! You listen to me! Can you even hear me?

He focuses on the music, drowning out
the world and his mum's voice in it. It is
Annihilating Rhythm by UltraSonic, it's
his total favourite. That big euphoric piano
line that just belongs to a world that is just
not like this shitey boring shitey one that
he lives and breathes. Most of all he loves
the sound of the crowd. He loves how they
keep in the sound of crowd. The sound of it
sends a secret thrill to his stomach making
him feel tiny and exposed and terrified and
vulnerable and excited all at once. Kind
of like the feeling he used to get when he
was about ten years old and Spanner would
boastfully show him those pictures of naked
ladies that he kept in his bedroom. Tuning in
to the sound of that cheering dancing crowd
he tries to imagine that he is there with them.
And pretty soon he will be.

His spine tingles.

His throat tightens.

Spanner's coming round later. Spanner's
coming round later in his mate's car. And for
the first time ever, he's taking Johnno to an
actual proper rave.

So Mum can just go and get fucked.

Before long, there are two toots on the car
horn outside, Johnno stands bolt upright
and still, hesitating for one second, before
making a bolt for it, out the door, past his
shouting Mum, hood up, down the stair, and
straight in to the back of Spanner's mates car.
A screech of the tyres, a shout of *awright wee
man* and they're off.

Where we headed to?

7.

Robert Dunlop listens to the windscreen
wipers beat their lethargic steady rhythm.
The sort of the drizzle that seems in all
honesty like it just can't be arsed trying.

Welcome to Motherwell. Where even the
rain has given up the ghost.

Time to get out of here, move on. The
commute into Glasgow was getting to be a
right pain in the arse. If only he could find
the time, put his mind to it, he'd get a wee
place in the city. Promotion was just around
the corner, he was sure of it, the extra money
would help. One day, eventually, soon even,
he'd move. He would.

Never one for sticking things out were you
son?

And what's that supposed to mean Dad?

You know exactly what I mean Robert, don't
give me that.

Ach, shut it you old fart.

Robert had lived in Motherwell his whole
life. His dad, like so many others, had got
a job at Ravenscraig steelworks in 1954
when the labour force expanded. When
he'd finished school, a teenager, Robert
had joined the same workforce at first. A
steelman, just like his old man. He was there
during the strikes in 1980 after the Tories
got in, he was out there picketing, leafleting,
the lot. He was into all that stuff once, just
like everyone else was, we all go through it.
Except you couldnae let it alone could you
Dad?

We won then, son. We won in 1980.

Things were changing though Dad. Things were changing and had you to keep up. You knew it yourself. You said when they went after the miners, you said it would be us next.

I always said we should have supported the miners. If we had then maybe

Maybe nothing. You saw the way it was going. You're supposed to get wise as you get older, Dad. You're supposed to get sensible. If you want to help your community you find a more practical way of doing it.

Like joining the police force, you mean?

Well exactly. Fucking exactly. Linwood. Bathgate. Gartcosh. Ravenscraig. Monuments to an old way of thinking. Those old certainties were dying Dad, just like you were, and you knew it even back then.

It's called solidarity Robert. Solidarity. Togetherness. The sort of mentality that says, see me and you, we're the same. What's good for you is good for me. A sort of collective empathy. That's what they were trying to destroy, son.

It's called pissing into the wind, Dad. There was to be no stopping it.

You're no listening, that's no the point. It was a fight for an understanding of who we are, of what we are. Of what we should be.

And if you want to know who won that fight, Dad, take a look around. Maybe if you'd still been here to see it all finally come crashing down you'd have understood. It's pointless trying to imagine anything beyond the facts of what you can see around you. Scorched earth, Dad. Scorched fucking earth.

It had been two years since the plant was demolished. He tunes into the radio. Some news thing. Seemed that constant background noise was necessary these days to get a bit ay fucking peace.

Some believe that unless stronger action is taken by the government these young people will continue to be a danger to themselves and to the rest of society. If the proposed Criminal Justice Bill becomes law it will grant police and local authorities increased powers to shut down these 'raves' which many are increasingly seeing as an anti-social problem. But don't young people have a right to party? And if the government is allowed to restrict their civil liberties, might not ours be next?

Aye, thinks Robert. A wee place in the city. That'd be nice. Somewhere in the country maybe. Maybe get a dog. Something like that.

8.

They've been driving for a couple of hours now.

It wasn't supposed to be this far away.

Spanner's mate, the driver, is called something like Dennis or Derek, but Johnno has completely forgotten his actual name already due to his own insistence on calling himself the D-Man, or D-Day, or D-Funk, or D-Mob, or D-Dog, or D-Bomb, or other combinations of his own first initial and a seemingly randomly selected noun.

D-Person is trying to act like everything is cool, while Spanner gets increasingly irate. Johnno, trying to hide his growing nerves, stays quiet. And still.

What do you mean you're sure? How sure is sure?

Listen geeza we're on the right track now I'm telling ya.

D-Guy was seemingly from somewhere in the south of England, though Johnno had been unable to engage him in normal conversation for long enough to find out what exactly he was doing in Livingston.

Call the number. Call the number again.

From where, you think I just carry a phone around like some yuppy?

Stop at the next services, use a fuckin payphone or sumhin, here, fuckin, gie me the number, an fuckin, I'll dae it.

Spanner had explained to Johnno how it worked. He had a mate, presumably the D-Laddie here, who in turn had a mate who knew someone who worked in a record store in Glasgow where you would go to pick up the number for this big free party happening out of town. All you had to do was call that number and they'd tell you exactly where it was.

It's all about keeping it on the down-low, Spanner had said. You game for it wee man? It'll be proper. The whole plan is in place eh an nuhin can possibly go wrong.

And what you gonna say to them exactly: excuse me mate I'm at a service station off the motorway in the arse end of fucking nowhere – you heard of it by any chance? Can you give me directions from there? We already know where it is you twat.

Well how are we no there yet then?

We missed the turning and now we're going back I'm telling ya, I'm fucking on top of it alright! Tunes, we need some fucking tunes.

Spanner fiddles with the radio tuner.

And if the government is allowed to restrict their civil liberties, might not ours be next?

Not that for fucksake!

D-Baws fumbles around for a tape he likes and thrusts it into Spanner's hand, who resentfully slams it in and hits play.

They sit. Listening.

Johnno pipes up.

What…what is this?

This my son, is Autechre. You like it?

Put on sumhin a bit more bouncin man

No, I, like it, it's, it's…different…it's cool.

Yes mate, listen to that beat yeah… Criminal Justice And Public Order Bill. You know about this yeah?

Johnno nods, although in truth he's not quite sure.

What they are trying to do yeah is outlaw raves. Criminalise the party scene yeah. So what they're saying they want to do is make it illegal to have a big outdoor party with, and this is a quote, music characterised wholly or predominantly by the emission of a succession of repetitive beats. Yeah? So Autechre, what they did yeah, was they recorded this track where no bars contain identical beats. This track has no, by definition, no repetitive beats. You could have a big fuck off party and listen to nothing but this track and they'd have to let ya! It'd be totally fucking legal and they'd have to fucking let ya!

Aye it'd be pure murder but.

Shut up Spanner. This is what I'm talking about yeah, it's like music as a political act. They try to persecute us but we become radical by necessity!

Oh for fucksake will you gie at rest ya wally?

Fuck off Spanner, listen to the D-Boy! What I'm saying is yeah like rock n' roll and the music of our parents' generation, it was all

31

narrative and linear, and icon hero worship but this, this is different. This about a pulse yeah, it's a living thing, a living pulse, yeah, and they can't kill it.

It's a fuckin tune! A record! No even a very good one. Aws it is is, it doesnae mean… nuhin. Nuhin. Awright? Noo let's just get to this fuckin party, an fuckin, get on wi it. For fucksake!

It doesn't mean nothing? It doesn't mean nothing! You need to radicalise yourself Spanner. You hear me? Radicalise yourself mate. Radicalise!

Shut. The Fuck. Up!

And so it continued. Johnno had stopped listening, he didn't really understand what Spanner's weird mate was on about anyway. A living pulse. Whatever. Instead he tunes in to this new music, willing it to calm his apprehensive heart. A living pulse. He focuses on that soft repetitive melody, and as he stares at his own shady reflection in the window he begins to imagine that melody as his own living pulse. Visualising it like liquid flowing through his veins. And he imagines it as the living pulse of the tarmac, and the electricity pylons that flick past his eyes keeping time. And of the streaky beads of rain catching and refracting the sparkle of passing headlights as they slide along the window, clinging on to the glass for dear life.

9.

Fucksake Johnno.

Fucksake.

Maybe she should just go to bed.

No. No, she should wait up.

Fuck.

She fiddles with radio.

these 'raves' which many are increasingly
seeing as an anti-social problem. But don't
young people have a right to party? And if
the government is allowed to restrict their
civil liberties, might not ours be next?

No. Not that. That's not what she wants to
listen to at all, shite, change it. What else is
there? Best of the Eighties? Fuck. Best of the
Eighties it is. Ok. Shit.

Young people have a right to and for this and
that. She never had a right. She was pretty
sure nobody ever asked her about her rights.

Lists. Where were her lists? Ironing. Ok.
Might as well get started on the bloody
ironing.

The wee shit.

She'd really, really tried to make the world
that he came into a safe one, and a happy
one, and one that he could be thankful for
and it's no perfect alright. Alright Johnno?
It's no perfect but it was hard bloody work
just to keep things ticking over, without you
running off and making it look like I cannae
even cope, and this is the fucking thanks…

The things she should do when she sees him.

Ground him. Tick.

Slap him. Tick.

Scream.

Oh she could scream. But she doesn't. She just stands behind the ironing board. Rooted. Frozen. As still as furniture.

The song on the radio is Aztec Camera's *Somewhere In My Heart*.

It's no perfect this, but it was the best I could do. And it's all I've got, just this wee flat and you. Son.

Batter him. Tick.

Strangle him. Tick.

Hug him.

Just, hug him.

Tick. Tick, tick, tick, tick.

In a wee living room, in a tiny flat in Livingston, clutching a clothes iron firmly in her left hand and staring at the pattern on the wallpaper, wide-eyed and empty-stomached, while on the radio some young men from East Kilbride sing about walking down love's motorway, singing hearts and flowers, and a star above the city in the northern chill. Standing there, completely still, Alison McCreadie thinks about her son. And for the first time in years, she begins to cry.

10.

At some point up the road as the bickering continues, the D-Man takes what he hopes is the right turning, and slows down as they come into a small country road in suspiciously heavy traffic.

This looks like sumfink.

The slow traffic comes to a sudden standstill. Someone up ahead has stopped for a piss. Other male passengers, having presumably been driving some distance too, see the window of opportunity and hurl themselves through it, and they all follow suit. A winding line of traffic at a standstill pierced by multiple simultaneous arcs of silvery uriney gold in the moonlight, like a punctured garden hose.

Spanner looks around. Lads. We're in the right place.

D-Bag lets out a big laugh and starts rhythmically pumping the car horn and banging his head to his own beat.

And so they arrive.

It's dark where they dump the car but they can hear noise and see some kind of tent thing up ahead. It looks smaller, and a bit shiter, than the ones Johnno's heard about. The ground is damp and muddy and the air is cold. They're about to start heading over when Johnno feels Spanner warmly take his hand.

Here. You'll need one ay these.

Spanner takes his hand away. Johnno looks down at his own palm and sees a big round white pill with a picture of something that looks like a star cut into it. He looks back up to Spanner, who is smiling.

Are you taking one?

Am takin one aye. I've got another for later if you want.

Johnno is silent.

Dinnae listen to the scare stories fae school, Johnno, eh. You're fine. It's fine. Mostly, see when sumhin bad happens it's just cos ay the water. Just cos ay drinkin too much water. Go easy on the water and you'll be fine.

Like a Strong?

What?

Eh, like a Strong. Remember. When we used to fill up a glass with diluting juice, and no water. A Strong. It's better if you go easy on the water, it's more…fun.

…Aye. Aye, like a Strong. Nice one Johnno. Cool.

Johnno looks at his hand again. But this isn't like a Strong though. This isn't even like the time Spanner got detention for crushing up the blackboard chalk and snorting it up his nose. This is it.

He looks around at the mud and grass, and feels a chill around his cheeks as he stares forwards at the unspectacular and uninviting tent up ahead. It'll never be like it was, that's what they always said. All those magazines that Spanner lent him always said the raving scene is over, it's sold out and moved on, it's not the same, it's in the past now, it's changed. It's been done.

But it's not been done by me.

Everyone's always talking about the past and saying that right now is shite. Just empty and shite. And they're probably right too. But what's left then? What's left for me?

Fuck it.

Fuck the lot ay them.

11.

Johnno feels nothing at first.

They're skirting round the edges of the dancing crowd in the tent. Johnno feels out of place, uncovered, like he's come wearing the wrong clothes to the school dance.

Maybe Spanner's been done. Maybe someone's sold him a paracetamol or something. That'd be just like him eh. That'd be just like the thing. The relief at the thought outweighs the disappointment.

Are you sure these are real Spanner?

Course they're fuckin real, just gie it a minute.

———————

Scorched earth, Dad. Scorched fucking earth.

These words still echo in Robert's mind as he steps through the doors of Finnieston police station, and the Super says to him: it's been a while since you've hud tae use your storm trooper gear eh PC Dunlop?

Aye, it is aye.

Still mind your riot control training alright?

Aye, aye I do, aye.

Well. Just as fucking well.

———————

These are never real Spanner. You've been done ya dick. Fuckin paracetamol or something I bet ye.

Fuckin shut it Johnno. You'll see.

And then. Sure enough.

The rush sneaks up on him. It starts with a
sort of fuzzy jelly warm ache in the legs and
the torso and before spreading up the back
of the neck like an electric waterfall flowing
backwards, mainlining to his brain. He feels
like he might fall over, like he might throw
up at any moment but it's still, glorious.
Feeling like he needs to sit down he leans
into Spanner who puts his arm round him.

Are you alright mate?

Johnno looks up at his friend, a weird
conspiratorial smile cracking across his face.
He breathes out loudly and pulls him in for a
hug, a warm glow pulsing through his body,
a sort of blissful golden effervescence like
he's got champagne for blood. His mate, his
best mate squeezes his body tight and starts
to laugh. Glorious. Fucking glorious.

Holy shit Spanner man, holy fuck. Fuck.

Spanner keeps laughing and so does Johnno
and for a while they both just stand there
holding each other and laughing. D-Guy
who has been watching the dancing crowd
with a kind of desperate impatience turns
round and noticing instantly what has
happened throws his hands behind his head
and shouts out yeeeeeeessss and lunges
towards them. To Johnno's surprise he starts
massaging their necks with each of his hands,
big smile beaming. Johnno loves it but. The
massage. The touch. He really really loves it.

———————

Robert surveys his equipment:

Helmet – check

Steel capped boots – check

Body armour – check

Harness, including radio, cuffs, CS spray – check

Baton – check

Safe. It's aw designed to make you totally safe.

He feels strangely outside of his own body.

Robert. You're safe.

Just some kids. Just some daft kids having a party in a field. I mean, aw this, seems a bit much really doesn't it.

Aye it does, Robert, aye it bloody well does.

Fuck off Dad naebody asked you.

———————

Weaving in and out of dancing bodies they make their way into the crowd, passing the faces of all the dancers, kids like them, older folks who look like they work in an office or could be a younger teacher, girls with dreadlocks like Johnno's never seen, all together moving, every one ensnared in the rhythm, their faces some contorted, lost in music, but each one fucking beautiful. They catch his eye and he feels he understands them. He feels them see him. A gleeful, fleeting, wordless, exchange: welcome son. Welcome.

And without even noticing the music finds
a flow through him, speaking straight to
his body. Like it's flowing through him
but like he's immersed in it at the same
time, engulfing him in its immediacy, in its
intimacy. And the rushing stops and he locks
into a groove and hits a blissful plateau,
his own body a tiny brick in a wall of
sweating muscle, for hours. Hours. Slipping
effortlessly between individual interactions
and a sort of tribal mass consciousness. All
of us, he thinks. All of us together holding
on, clinging on for dear life! Knowing that
the world outside is shit but all there really is
is us! And all that really exists is now, right
now! And surely, surely to fuck the drugs are
just part of the glue that binds us together,
and what we're rushing off, what we're really
rushing off is each other.

———————

You ready for some action then?

Robert rubs his sweaty hands on the rough,
thick, tough canvas of his blue overalls and
looks up at the officer opposite him.

Aye uh huh.

Show the wee scumbags who the fucking
boss is.

Super says it's precautionary.

What was that?

Precautionary measure

What?

Oh, eh. Nothing.

Johnno's sense of time and space is lost.
Could be five minutes or an hour since he
last saw Spanner. But he's never felt less
alone and so he's not scared. Not scared one
bit.

Some water wee man?

No, had enough thanks. Go easy on the
water. It's more fun without it. Like a Strong
right. Like a fucking Strong, eh?

Robert clenches his teeth.

The squad are laughing slapping backs,
psyching up for the bust.

His throat dries and tightens.

Has anyone eh, has anyone got a drink ay
water?

I love you man I mean it.

I really love you.

Where's Spanner. Who's Spanner? Aw he's
my mate. He's my mate, have you seen him?

All of us holding on together, eh.

I fucking love you man.

It doesn't mean nothing, that's what he said.
He said it doesn't mean nothing. But it does
but. It is real. It fuckin is though. Well but
what if we just pretend that it's real. Imagine.

Imagine that it is. What then? What would we have then, eh?

Fucking hell you're tripping wee man.

———————

Radios crackle. Orders are given. Briefings are made.

We have tried to move them on peacefully but there has been resistance.

Resistance? What kind of resistance?

Well. They've had their chance. Ok. Well.

They're breaking the law, well. We are the law. They're breaking the law and they're refusing to stop.

We're here to keep things right, make sure everyone's, kept, safe.

Well then. Fucking well then!

Let's go! Let's fucking do this!

———————

Spanner? Have you seen Spanner?

Johnno staggers exhausted and weak at the knees, to pause for a moment to catch his breath. In his misty consciousness he feels a tremor through the crowd. A panic, a fear. His body is tossed around as the crowd begins to scatter. He forces his body through the crowd, propelling forwards in aimless manic, physical hysteria

———————

Get back! Get back! Get back! Get back!

Robert hears these words come tumbling out his mouth like they're being said by someone else.

The crowd begins to scatter. Scattering like dogs.

Feral. Out of control.

Some of them try to push back. To fight back. Adrenalin courses through his veins, his own animal instincts kicking in.

It's fight or flight. Fight or fucking flight, right?

Out of the corner of his eye he sees a figure in a green hoody charging towards him. In one instant trained reflex he reaches for his baton and raises it high above his head

———————

The last thing Johnno is aware of before the weapon comes crashing down, is the sudden sight of a row of shields, of stamping boots, charging, shouting, beating, and a voice ringing in his ears screaming

POOOOOOOLLLLLIIIIIIIIIIIICCEEEE!

12.

Where, is, he?

13.

Jeeeeeessuus fuck.

Johnno hurts. In every way, he hurts.

He looks around at the rows of dejected souls, gurning jaws, confused and frightened faces; ghostly white skin, pasty and damp and reptilian.

Those wide gaping eyes which once looked so mighty and angelic now just look desperate, childlike and lost, like the panicked dead eyes of fish flapping out of water, under the cold neon strip lights of the Finnieston police station foyer.

Fucking hell. I know how these munters feel.

The pain of the beating throbs dull and warm in the side of his face and deep in his shoulders. He shivers.

Later, much, much later, when his body has grown and changed, sitting at home while the television shows a mass of young people, students, breaking into Millbank tower and an onscreen voice argues that they can't be allowed to run around wild, they need to be taught a lesson, John McCreaddie, 31 years old will become suddenly aware of an echo through his muscles, a brief pain in his right shoulder. And for the first time in years he'll remember sitting in the police station foyer feeling vulnerable, lost, deeply alone, and quite, quite scared.

But that's later. Much, much later.

Oh fuck fuck fuck. His bones feel like they could turn to dust, his throat is parched, he wants to be sick but there is nothing inside. What happens now?

I've been hearing stories Johnno, about those boys.

Aye, Mum.

That Scott Smith is a bad laddie, Johnno.

You don't even know him, Mum.

Wanting nothing more than to crawl into somewhere warm and make the whole bright, hostile, world just disappear he pulls his green hoody up tight around his ears, clenches his eyes tight shut, and tries, to focus on, to remember, what he was doing before aw this. Before he followed that fucking dafty Spanner down this rabbit hole of shite.

Zelda. He was playing fucking Zelda.

If this was Zelda right now, he'd know exactly what to do, he'd know every right turn, every secret passageway that you need to escape the dungeon. If this was Zelda, he'd even know about a secret door that leads to a special treasure chest. And you'd open it, the treasure chest and there would be a wee red heart inside. And you'd grab it, the heart, and that would make your health go up. He pictures a broken, empty, shell of a heart filling up to the top till it glows hot, and bright, and red. He could use some of that action the now. A total fucking beezer.

Zelda V: The Adventures of Johnno – an illegal rave fairytale!

He breathes in deep. And opens his eyes.

Fuck.

14.

Spanner wakes up, face down in mud, with
his T-shirt caked in his own sick.

Fucksake man aw naw.

Johnno? Johnno where are ye? Ya wee dick.

Fuck am ah outside fur? Fucks happenin here
man aw naw

Later it'll begin to come back to him. The
drive oot, the party, getting separated fae
wee Johnno. The polis arriving, the mad
bolt for it when the crowd turned nasty,
escapin doon the road an keepin the party
goin wi two, was it two lads fi, fuck knows,
in the back ay a van somewhere and must ay
stumbled back up the road tay…here.

Just ootside the D-man's motor. Tidy.

Later still, in a week or so, when he sees wee
Johnno after school, he'll hear aboot how
the wee man got knocked aboot by the fuzz.
Got a blow tae the cheek fae the butt ay a
stick like that – doosh – and then another
swipe – wap – like that back across the
shooders. He'll see Johnno's bruises and he'll
look at the wee man a wee bit different. Sort
ay impressed, eh. But wi a sort ay, sadness
an aw, for sumhin, lost. Mibbe. He'll hear
aboot how Johnno got taken tae a station an
how he pure shat it cos he thought he was in
for it but how they'd actually just called his
maw who came and picked him up but by
the sounds ay hings that had actually been
the worst bit. He'll hear aboot how Johnno's
maw says that if she ever sees the two ay
them hingin aboot thegither ever again she'll

fuckin actually kill the baith ay thum so noo
they've got tay be pure sly aboot hingin
aboot noo. Later on, eh. Later on he'll find
out aw ay this.

Because right now the only things in the
whole world that Scott Spanner Smith
knows about are the bright morning light,
the freezing cold air, the deep aching pain of
body and soul, and the cold, bitty remains
of yesterday's Pot Noodle stuck behind his
teeth.

15.

Robert's left eye twitches slightly, as his hands grip the steering wheel. There were no too many problems. The Super had said that was a good bust. Textbook.

His bleary eyes blink in the daylight. He'd forgotten how long it took for the adrenalin to leave the system.

There was this kid. This wee laddie. Looked only about 15. Robert had seen him, sitting there in the station, green hoody too big for him pulled up, wee bony face poking out, eyes shut. Purple bruise across the side of his cheek. He'd seen him, and he'd recognised him. He recognised him from the bust.

And he had stood, unable to take his eyes off the kid, as he remembered: a swift blow down with the butt, a swipe across the back. Two beats. Textbook.

The boy was dripping in sweat and looked, so, light, so fragile. But, other-worldly, almost. Serene. What did he know that Robert didn't?

He recognised him, aye, but this was the first time, he knew, that he'd really seen him.

Later, years later, when Robert Dunlop is still commuting from Motherwell and any real thoughts of significant promotion have disappeared into the rear view mirror as he edges his way towards retirement; when this brief encounter with the green hooded boy is left obscured under the gathering dust of decisions, and convictions, ground out over a lifetime, Robert will come to remember

Johnno quite differently. He'll remember seeing a savage, unruly youth. A hooligan. A yob.

But that was later. Much, much later.

What are they playing at these kids, eh?

They're a danger to themselves. Out of control. Was never like that in my day. It's a disgrace, really, it's, it's disruptive to local communities is what it is, it's, no right.

Robert. What is it you're so afraid of, son?

Fuck off Dad! You cannae just let them run around wild. Ok? Come on, they need to learn! They need to be taught a lesson, or else what will we have?

Or else what will have.

He glances into the rear view mirror.

Anyway. Must remember to look intay they shares. National Power and Powergen wasn't it. Probably stop at the chemists an aw pick up something to help me sleep.

Fucking night shifts man.

I could really use a good night's rest.

16.

Johnno folds his bruised and aching frame deep into the corner of the back seat of his mum's car.

What. A. Downer.

Alison stares straight ahead. Determined no to make eye contact in the rear view mirror. Determined no to let him off the hook, determined to make him feel as terrible, as helpless as she had done.

She sneaks a glance.

Look at him. Swollen face, what had they done to him?

She clenches her teeth, and flicks on the indicator switch. Tick, tick, tick, tick…

Johnno, not daring to look up at his mum, stares out the window at the passing streets as they make their way on to the motorway.

Men in suits, bankers maybe, aggressively commanding the pavements on their way to work.

An old man lying on a bench, covered in newspapers.

A street corner with three different bookies on it with their shutters down.

And onto the motorway, a cavalcade of concrete, petrol and steel, carrying hundreds of different people, different lives, along in the same direction, passing each other out, never noticing as they sail by in their individual little pods.

Shut off from the world, separate.

This is it. This is all there is.

That's your lot, really.

But that was Spanner talking surely. Where was he? He'd be fine. He'd managed worse, Johnno was sure.

He watches the early morning sun reflecting off the passing road signs. Bouncing repetitive rays of light, momentarily cross the inside of his mum's car, catching her cheekbone, his hand, the metal piece on that seatbelt. A fleeting glimmer.

He feels a tingle through the back of his neck. Was that residual drugs in his bloodstream, the morning cold, or, what? And almost before his mind can catch up he feels his body remembering, and imagining.

And he imagines huge, pulsating crowds.

He imagines a tingle in his spine.

He imagines an electric waterfall.

And he imagines, and remembers, togetherness; a sort of collective empathy and see me, see you, we're the same, what's good for you is good for me, I'm for you, so welcome son. Welcome.

Later, when he sees him next week after school, he'll try to explain all this to Spanner and Spanner will tell him that he's an arsehole, that it's no real. The drugs fast track the chemicals that produce all that stuff to trick you. That's why it ruins your brain, that's why you feel like shite for so long after. You're using up all of next week's happiness in one night.

But that's later.

Right now, staring out at the bleakness of the urban morning Johnno keeps his eyes wide open this time and lets it all play out against his weary retina. Speeding over the concrete river of the motorway he sees the world, his world at the close of the twentieth century, and he sees himself in it. He feels a flickering warmth inside his cold, exhausted body. A tiny glow. An empty heart shell, fills up, throbbing bright and red and hot. A living pulse. It beats and beats and beats and beats and beats and beats and beats.

He looks up at his mum, and bravely, hopefully, tries to catch her eye.

Later, back at home, when she's helping Johnno painfully lift up his arms to remove his green hoody, Alison will softly run her fingers along the purple bruises across the top of his back. He'll take her hand, and say: it's ok mum. I'm ok.

She'll look at him, and say: I know.

But that's later.

As the world flickers past the window Johnno thinks about home; the familiar streets, the school building that he can see from his bedroom window. But he imagines something else as well. Something beyond the facts of what he can see around him. Beyond the bricks and mortar of his school, the bitumen roads, the orange sulphur streetlights, the dog shit. An idea. An understanding of who we are, of what we are. Of what we could be.

And he holds on to it. Because nobody can arrest his imagination.

Sitting in the back seat of his mother's car, with her staring straight ahead refusing to look at him, refusing to talk to him, wanting to scream at him but secretly, underneath it all just deeply, deeply glad that he's alive, sitting there with his head aching and his body sick and weak and broken, with his blood flowing dirty through his veins, with his eyes wide open and his bruised cheek pressed hard against the cold glass, Johnno McCreadie, 15 years old, green hoody and spotty skin, sits turning the same phrase over and over and over in his head. A small smile melts across his weary face.

It doesn't mean nothing.
It doesn't mean nothing.
It doesn't mean nothing.
It doesn't mean nothing.
It doesn't mean nothing.
It doesn't mean nothing.
It doesn't mean nothing.
It doesn't mean nothing.
It doesn't mean nothing.
It doesn't mean nothing.
It doesn't mean nothing.
It doesn't mean nothing.
It does *not* mean *nothing*.

Appendix
List of tracks used in the original production

The Orb
Little Fluffy Clouds

The Prodigy
Their Law

Aphex Twin
Alberto Balsam

Koji Kondo
The Legend of Zelda: a Link to the Past, Title Theme

Aphex Twin
Blue Calx

Ultrasonic
Annihilating Rhythm

Aphex Twin
Heliosphan

Autechre
Flutter

Leftfield
Song of Life

Josh Wink
Higher State of Consciousness

Human Resource
Dominator

Chemical Brothers
Playground For A Wedgeless Firm

Autechre
444

The Prodigy
Weather Experience

CHALK FARM

by Kieran Hurley and AJ Taudevin

9781783190218

Maggie is just in from Sainsbury's Local to make a quick sandwich for Jamie. He likes his cheese and pickle. With the crusts off. A good heart, that lad. Not like those other boys around here. You know what boys are like. Laws unto themselves once they reach that age. But it's those other boys, really. Not Jamie. A boy with a Batman lunch box? What harm is he to anybody?

Co-written by AJ Taudevin and Kieran Hurley, *Chalk Farm* explores love, responsibility, and the culture of blame and retribution surrounding the 2011 English riots.

'the writing is brilliant, sharp, poetic, passionate, full of searing insight into the politics of blame, matched with a brilliant eye for the detail of life in divided Britain today.'
Joyce McMillan, *Scotsman*

WWW.OBERONBOOKS.COM

Follow us on www.twitter.com/@oberonbooks
& www.facebook.com/oberonbook